Job Interview Techniques

The Essentials

Andrew William James

CONTENTS

Introduction

"All our dreams can come true if we have the courage to pursue them"

Walt Disney

To achieve great things in life or to make ourselves content with our achievements, we need to understand we can only achieve things for ourselves by ourselves.

There are no magic formulas and most people do not win the lottery. Those people who do achieve success do this because of their hard work rather than by luck.

And so it is with finding a new job, only you can make it happen, no one else can do this for you.

Before becoming a Career Coach, I spent many years in both the private and public sectors and have interviewed well over 1500 people for roles.

I believe that any Interview is just as much about the Interviewee interviewing the organisation and interviewer, as it is about the interviewer, interviewing the interviewee.

This guide will not deal with how to write and present your Curriculum Vitae (CV), since it is assumed that as you have an interview your CV reads well.

This short guide is based on my own experiences and designed to offer the reader a last-minute or "night before" guide to doing the very best they can at an Interview.

Researching your prospective employer

"It is wiser to find out than to suppose"

Mark Twain

As much as an Interview is about the Interviewer selecting the right candidate, the interview is also about the Interviewee making an informed decision as to whether or not the Organisation is a good fit for him or her.

These are the 10 questions I suggest you have in the back of your mind, and you should seek answers to, during an interview:

- Is this organisation a good fit for me? / Will I be happy working here?
- Is this job going to benefit me in the long term?
- Am I likely to stay in this role for at least two years?
- What are the people like at the organisation, do I feel any synergy with the interviewer?
- Is the organisation financially stable?

- What is the employee feedback of the organisation?
- What is the customer perception of the organisation?
- Are the salary and perks good?
- If I get offered the job, will I accept it?
- Are there any warning bells ringing?

Let us examine each question in turn.:

Is this organisation a good fit for me? / Will I be happy working here?

You may have spent time researching an Organisation and be happy that this is the right place for you, you agree with the ethics and what they stand for. If you have not done this then you need to do this before the interview. Google the Organisation and examine their website. Look at the profiles of their senior staff, see if there is any negative press in the papers. If you are happy the Organisation is a good fit for you, then ask yourself if you think you will be happy at this workplace.

We spend so much of our lives at work that it is crucial to our physical and mental wellbeing that we are happy with the organisation and the people we work with. There is nothing worse than being unhappy at work, it affects us all far more mentally than we at first perceive.

So now is the time to ask that question, if you do not know the answer just yet then gain an impression during the interview. Being happy at work is just as important as earning a good salary. Some would say it is more important, however, this is very easy to say if you are financially secure.

Is this job going to benefit me in the long term?

In today's market people move from role to role frequently, however, each move should act to progress your career. If you are unhappy in your current role, it is all too easy to look for another job and take it on just to get out of your current situation. This can be a mistake, each move in your career needs to bring with it benefits. Each organisation you join should be for at least two years. Any shorter and you stand the danger of being classified as someone that moves from role to role too frequently and organisations will be cautious about investing in you.

Ideally, you should be looking for career progression within each role OR acquiring skills that will stand you in good stead for the future.

In my career, I decided in my teens that I wanted to work for a particular organisation. I researched the organisation to find out which IT systems they used. To get into the organisation, I studied subjects that I knew would be beneficial. When I started work, I targeted organisations that had similar IT systems to my dream workplace. I knew that once I had gained the skills and knowledge they were looking for, I stood a good chance of getting an interview and getting a job. This worked out well for me, although it took a lot longer than I anticipated, but does highlight the importance of making sure there is value in the roles you take and having a long-term plan.

Am I likely to stay in this role for at least two years?

There was a time when people used to stay in jobs forever. However, this has changed, and it is quite common to move from one organisation to another or even move around within organisations. Whether or not this will change again due to pension arrangements remains to be seen. As people get older, they tend to remain with employers offering excellent pension schemes and view staying put as a better alternative to starting new pensions. Most recruiters are looking for stability and a good steady career progression. This would present itself as:

2009 – 2011 Trainee Salesperson 1st Organisation

2011 – 2012 Junior Salesperson 2nd Organisation

2012 – 2014 Senior Sales Executive 3rd Organisation

2014 – 2016 Sales Manager 4th Organisation

2016 – 2018 Area Manager 5th Organisation

In the above example, our salesperson has stayed for four years in the 1st organisation, moving slowly up and then moved to a more senior role, which they stayed in for two years and then again two more times. This is normal behaviour and there is a progression pattern. As an interviewer, this is what you would want to see, and it is easy for the interviewee to explain their progression.

Everyone makes mistakes and whilst it is fine to have one or two short stays within several years, which are easy to explain away, it becomes more difficult if there are several short stays. If you have several short stays, be prepared to be questioned. The fact you have got an interview is great, but most likely you will be asked to talk through your CV and having worked out your story beforehand, you are less likely to have to endure further questioning.

What are the people like at the organisation, do you feel any synergy with the interviewer?

To be happy and productive at work, we must get on with not only our colleagues but also our managers. If you do not get on with them, then you will be more likely to want to change jobs.

One way of finding if there is synergy with your interviewer is to observe body language. Is your Interviewer displaying open body language such as uncrossed legs and arms? These suggest your interviewer is open and receptive and wants to engage in conversation. Crossed arms and legs convey the opposite. Facial expressions are of course an instant giveaway.

Another way of seeing if there is synergy between you and this prospective workplace is to see how people are dressed, are they wearing the same sort of clothes you would wear to work and feel comfortable in or are they completely different? Can you identify with them? It is human nature to get on with people having the same or similar tastes to ourselves. If you feel comfortable in a suit and tie but can see everyone else is in Jeans and a T-Shirt, you must ask yourself if this organisation is a good fit. If you are open to change then fine but if not, will you just feel awkward and out of place?

Trawling social media will reveal a lot about your future employer. Just as some organisations research potential employees, so too should employees research their prospective employer. LinkedIn is a great place to start, you can easily gain an understanding of who will be interviewing you, where they have worked and their level of experience.

Is the organisation financially stable?

The financial stability of your prospective employer is one of the key factors in deciding whether or not you accept a job. If your prospective employer is not financially stable, you could end up not being paid and out of a job with no redundancy payment.

In the private sector, you can make some background checks by googling the organisation, looking them up on companies' house and generally asking around. If you can get hold of their financial statements, it may be worth asking someone who can interpret these sheets to have a look for you.

A good indicator of how well an organisation is performing is to look at its balance sheet for the debt-to-equity ratio. This is Total Liabilities divided by Total Shareholder funds. There is no right or wrong answer here, but it will provide you with an indicator of whether the organisation has borrowed heavily. Another indicator is the "Current Ratio" This is Current Assets divided by Current Liabilities. For this calculation you would hope that the ratio will be more than 1, this means that the organisation can pay all its debts without resorting to having to borrow money. Try running these tests against similar size organisations you know are doing well, this will give you something to compare them with.

In the public sector, it's not so obvious as organisations are backed by the government. I would still do my research and look at what others are saying about the organisation on the internet alongside googling minutes from public meetings.

If an organisation is losing money and customers, then it's not a good choice of employer.

At the time of writing (Jan 2022) In the UK you must have been legally employed by an employer for 24 months before you are entitled to Statutory Redundancy Pay.

From April 6, 2018, the cap for weekly SRP is £508,

the maximum an employee can receive is £15,240. Employees are entitled to half a week's pay for each full year under the age of 22. For employees aged between 22 and 40, this is one week's pay for each full year and if you are 41 or older you are entitled to one and a half weeks' pay for each full year worked.

There are other types of redundancy such as contractual, whereby you may be entitled to more if it is in your contract of employment or voluntary redundancy.

What is the employee feedback of the organisation?

There are now many internet sites providing current and previous employees with the opportunity to comment on a workplace and give their feedback based on their experience. LinkedIn, Glassdoor etc. Be aware, disgruntled employees are likely to leave poor reviews and these may not be accurate. It is much better to find out what an organisation is like through someone who works there directly or second hand.

Good organisations receive glowing feedback from employees, they are proud to work for the organisation and not afraid to sing its praises. A poor organisation, on the other hand, will receive negative feedback from customers and employees. Employees are one of your best barometers in assessing whether or not an organisation is worth working for.

What is the customer perception of the organisation?

Imagine working for an Organisation in a sales capacity where the customer base is unhappy. I have worked for two organisations in the past with poor customer satisfaction ratings and it is incredibly stressful. Poor customer satisfaction is a huge barometer of the employee experience within a workplace. For example, an Organisation with good customer satisfaction is likely to be run by good managers with happy staff and thus together they create good customer satisfaction. An Organisation with poor customer satisfaction is more often than not run by poor or inexperienced managers, and this goes all the way to the top.

Sometimes these managers will blame the Product, their Staff, the Environment or even the Customers. These organisations are the type of organisations to avoid, and it is unlikely that without major restructures and the hiring of temporary consultants, they will turn things around. With this type of organisation, you are unlikely to stay for two years and with poor customer satisfaction comes poor financial stability.

You can check an Organisations satisfaction rating easily by googling them and looking at organisation satisfaction ratings.

Within the Public Sector, it is not as easy to ascertain how happy a customer is with their providers. I would start by finding out who the customers are, you could try approaching them for feedback. Or ask around the Recruitment Agencies.

Many Public Sectors have specialist reporting chronicles or websites. For example, the Health Sector has HSJ, the Health and Justice sector Justice Trends, Police, Police-Life.co.uk etc. These are good places to find out about the organisation you are interested in and if there is any negative feedback.

If a Public Sector organisation fails there is always the possibility of redeployment opportunities, but this is a lengthy process and you need to ask yourself if it is better to avoid working for the organisation in the first place, or, worth taking a chance in case it leads to something better.

Are the salary and perks good?

No matter what anyone says, a good salary is important, you need to make sure that the pay on offer is good and worth your while. Look at the perks the organisation is offering and decide if they are a good fit for you? It may be that whilst the salary is lower than you would like, the organisation is based in a city you want to live in where it is cheaper. In this case, one offsets the other. However, assuming this is not the case, it's important to negotiate a good salary deal at the outset as it's often harder to get a significant rise once you have joined than it is to start with.

This is particularly true in the Public Sector where traditionally salary levels have been lower than the Private Sector. The Public Sector however offers particularly good holiday entitlement, pension and where possible, flexible working. Bear in mind once you are on a salary level and grade, other than the statutory pay rises, promotion is through further interviewing. There is also the danger of the economy taking a downturn and public sector pay awards being frozen or the inevitable public sector re-organisation. So, you must start at a good level in the first place.

When looking at your overall remuneration, take into consideration any perks, Annual Leave, Expenses, Car, Gym Membership, Health Care etc. It all adds up and you may find an extra week's Annual Leave is worth more to you than an extra £500.

If I get offered the job, will I accept it?

Having investigated the organisation and the role, do you think you will accept an offer? It's important to go into the Interview either knowing 100% you will accept an offer, or you need further convincing that this is the right role for you.

If you have decided you will not accept the role but are curious, then go ahead, but you should be thinking if it is a waste of time for both you and the organisation and denying other candidates a fairer opportunity.

Are there any more warning bells ringing?

Warning Bells? Surely, we have covered everything. Unfortunately, not, there are still many more warning bells to be aware of.

Has the organisation made the proposed salary, or at least its range, and benefits clear?
Seek clarification on where you will be based and if

there is any travel involved.

There has been a trend resurging around Job Titles. Be wary of a role that has a great job title but low pay. Some companies will do this as a way of attracting people into roles they may not get in larger companies, but, that they think will impress the interviewee and attract them to the organisation. An example of this is say Director at a relatively small organisation as against going for a role of Senior Manager at a large, well-known organisation like Deloitte.

The role of Director sounds appealing but the organisation may be financially insecure, and you may be asked to undertake duties that are not commensurate with the level the title suggests.

Preparing for the Interview

"A mind troubled by doubt cannot focus on the course to victory"

Arthur Golden

Detox your Social Media

Some prospective employers will try and find out more about you before or after your interview by looking you up on social media. It is therefore important for you to clean up your social media image so that it presents the type of image you want your employer to see. If you have a lot of content that could be considered inappropriate in any way then consider removing some of the content, or, temporarily hibernating the account. Another option is to restrict who can see your accounts. Remember if you are not careful with your privacy it is not only you that an employer can see but your friends and associates.

A point that can be missed in tailoring your CV for a role is to make sure your LinkedIn profile matches that of your CV and that both are truthful. It is pointless making up job titles or exaggerating a position you once held as everything can be checked.

With so much of our lives available online, it is relatively easy for an employer to build a profile of potential employees, by the same token, it is just as easy vice versa.

Get your story straight

During your interview, you will either be asked to talk through your CV and experience, or you will be asked questions on it. You will create a better impression if you have rehearsed your storyline and have details such as dates, organisations, and roles to hand. When talking through your CV you must concentrate on the jobs you have had that closest match the job you are applying for. Do not spend time talking about your first job that is irrelevant. Instead, focus on the skills you have picked up in previous roles matching the requirements of the position you are applying for. The aim is to show you can bring something new to the table through your experience. Remember, as much as you may have enjoyed a role in the past, if it is not relevant the interviewer will not be interested. If the interviewer starts looking bored that's the time to move things on.

A large part of your story will be career progression and, as previously mentioned, you should have a good reason for moving from one role to the next. If there are any gaps in your employment think about what you did during those gaps (i.e., travelling, looking after someone, illness etc). In general, an interviewer will want to hear that you did something positive which helped you in your career or develop as a person.

Telepathy

Well maybe not quite telepathy, but you need to try and pre-empt the type of questions you are likely to be asked. If this position is new, then why is it new? has the organisation expanded, are they moving into a different field or are they combining posts and reducing staff. This is where research is vital. Try and think of the questions you are likely to be asked and work out your responses in advance.

You can get a good idea of the type of questions you may be asked by reading the company's Mission Statement, this will give you an idea of their values. Ensure that you have thoroughly checked the organisation's website, mission statement and its plans.

An example, if a company says it is committed to Net Zero in two years, then you may be asked for your opinions and ideas. Find out beforehand what they are doing to reduce their carbon footprint and use this in your response.

What to Wear

In most cases, the interviewer will expect you to wear smart business attire. Exceptions to this rule would be, for example, media-related industries.

I think you will have a good idea of what to wear and what not to wear. The important thing is you look fresh, natural and smart so that the interviewer can tell you have made an effort. Think ahead of the interview, if it is likely to be a warm day cut down the layers or ditch the overcoat, you do not want to appear hot and flustered. Remember not to wear too much perfume or aftershave as this can be overpowering. Makeup should be kept to what is necessary so that you create a good impression.

If your job requires you to dress casually, still consider dressing up for the interview. It will not go unnoticed. The golden rule here is that if you are in doubt, dress up not down.

Self-Affirmations

"You are braver than you believe, stronger than you seem, and smarter than you think."

A.A. Milne.

Actors portray an image of being confident and self-assured. The most successful people in business also portray images of self-confidence. How do they do this? they do this by telling themselves constantly they are great, god's gift, and can do anything they set their minds to.

When you think about it, this makes sense, the best

person to tell you, "You are great as you are", is, yourself. All too often we wait for other people to tell us we are great when the only person we need to hear this from is ourselves. Why wait for someone else to tell you what you already know?

Try writing down everything you are good at. Now read the list back to yourself while looking in a mirror. How does that feel? What's happening is you are reinforcing these positive messages in your mind, so, when you say them in an interview they flow convincingly and naturally. Repeat five to ten of your strongest self-affirmations daily and on the morning of your interview.

The Day of the Interview

"Always do your best, what you plant now you will harvest later."

Og Mandino

The day of the interview starts the night before, it is making sure you have a checklist and have everything in place for the next day. Having a checklist will mean you do not forget something key and panic in the morning. A checklist might look like this:

- Avoid Caffeine after lunchtime the day before the interview (this will make sure you're not kept awake the night before)
- Get Clothes, Shoes, Accessories ready
- Ensure that any papers you may need are packed
- Set Alarm Clock and backup alarm
- Ensure you have transport the next day, check train times, get a ticket if appropriate or if going by car, check route and make sure you have enough fuel
- Avoid any arguments, spicy food, limit or abstain

from alcohol

• Make sure you get a good night's sleep

On the morning of the interview try and wake up earlier than normal so you have time to wake up slowly and gently ease your way into the day. The goal here is not to rush around and make yourself panic. Waking early gives you time to have a shower, a proper breakfast and check your travel arrangement one more time before setting off.

Before your set off, check you have everything you need in your briefcase, rucksack or bag. This should include a copy of the Job Description and your CV, together with any written questions.

If you need to refer to these in the interview they are at hand. It helps to keep them in a folder so that the impression is that of being organised. It is also a good idea to take a bottle of water with you, more on that later.

Always, set off in plenty of time and aim to arrive early. If you get to the general area too early you can have a coffee and kill time whilst you wait. The point is you will be close by, on time, and relaxed. If you leave it late, you will be flustered and at worst will have missed the interview.

Aim to get to the building of your interview 10 – 15 minutes early, this gives you a chance to check out the building and gain some valuable first impressions, it also gives your interviewer a chance to prepare, and he or she will know you have made an effort to arrive on time.

First Impressions of your prospective employer

"First impressions matter. Experts say we size up new people in somewhere between 30 seconds and two minutes"

Elliot Abrams

You can gain a good first impression of an Organisation from the staff at the reception desk. Are they smart? Are they professional? Are they attentive to people who arrive or are they indifferent? Are they being asked to multitask and answer incoming phone calls?

Whilst the first impression you give your interviewer is important, so too is the first impression you get of your prospective employer.

Reception staff busy multitasking can be a sign that either the reception desk is not busy enough, so it makes sense they take on extra duties, or the organisation is having problems and asking staff to do more than one role. This becomes evident if reception staff are answering calls and ignoring visitors.

Depending on how much stress they are under will dictate how they treat you as a visitor.

Of course, there are exceptions to the rule, and it could be that you caught them on a bad day or the switchboard operator was off sick and they are having to cover. Either way, it's a first impression and one to take into consideration.

Other first impressions are the location of the building. If you intend to travel by public transport, does it have good bus, tube or train connections? If you intend to drive, are there convenient parking arrangements? There is nothing more frustrating than being late for work due to difficulties in travelling to your office and it is something which may cause you to look for another role before two years are up.

Take time to examine the outside of the building, has it been maintained, is it clean? This will tell you if the organisation has pride in where its employees are working. So too will the state of the reception area. Poor seating, lack of water and lack of conveniences are not appealing.

It's worth looking at how people are arriving and leaving and, it should be possible to distinguish between staff and clients. Do staff look relaxed and jovial, or do they look stressed, are they chatting to each other or rushing in? Do Clients or Customers look pleased to be visiting or do they look like they would rather be somewhere else? Is the reception area too clinical and devoid of any personality or is it warm and inviting?

All too often many organisations are proud to advertise their Diversity and Equality policies, but the biggest test of how successful and committed they are is what you see in their reception area. It is almost a showcase of what the organisation is like to work for. If you observe a reception desk at around 8.45 in the morning, when workforces typically arrive, you will get a pretty good idea of how diverse and happy employees are. People's attitudes and the way they behave in reception can give you a good idea of what the organisation is like to work for. If you get the job, it will be you walking in through that reception in a month.

Of course, now with COVID, physical interviews may be out of the question, so you should look for indicators instead in the interview panel or by querying policies if you have concerns.

Remember your Job interview is just as much about

you reviewing the organisation as the organisation reviewing you.

The Interview

"If you're going through hell, keep going"

Winston Churchill

So now you are in the hot seat, and it is your turn to create a good impression. From the moment you walk in through the door you will be judged and to some people that is quite off-putting. What you need to do is relax and not show you are nervous. Don't panic too much as most interviewers should be prepared for a small number of nerves and will look past this. If they don't then they are not getting the best from the interviewee.

To stop yourself from appearing nervous, start by gaining your first impression of the person or people interviewing you. Do they appear calm, relaxed, and inviting or have they adopted a stony face attitude? Do you think they will try and play good cop / bad cop – if so, which one will be the good cop and which will be the bad cop?

The first minute of entering the room is your chance

to create a great first impression.

Every interview is going to be different but the general rules are:

- Enter the room with your back straight and walk-in purposefully
- As you enter the room say "hello, good morning, afternoon or hi" – whichever comes naturally to everyone in the room and look them in the eye – do not look around while you are walking in.
- Shake hands purposefully, if someone stands first to shake hands then the rest will follow, if not then start with whoever is smiling or appears to be the most senior. Beware that some people do not shake hands and move on if this happens quickly. (Note that during COVID it is entirely reasonable not to shake hands and it may be that this continues for some time afterwards)
- Smile as this gives a good impression.

When sitting, sit down so you are comfortable, but in a way that your body language is open – do not cross your legs and arms if you can help it.

If you find it easier to take notes whilst the interview is in progress, ask if it is ok to do so, normally this is perfectly acceptable. Use the folder with your CV, JD, and Questions in it. Try not to refer to your CV during the interview as this will show that you are maybe not as familiar with it as you should be. If you do need to refer to your CV, then say something like "let me just check that date", but that should be a last resort.

During the interview there are several additional ways in which you can gain a better idea of the organisation and if it is right for you.

- Has your interviewer made an effort to dress smartly for you?
- Have they prepared properly; do they have the answers to all your questions?

Is the interviewer's body language open and friendly or is it guarded?

An Interviewer who has not prepared or dressed properly may not be taking the task as seriously as they should. In this situation, it may be up to you to find something to break the ice. Without being obvious and taking your eyes off the interviewer for too long, look around the room for any signs of the interviewer's personality.

Some people will give away their personalities in their offices, pictures of families, sports achievements, hobbies etc. If you see any clues, then use this as ammunition should you get the chance. You will know when the time is right as the conversation will have ceased and rather than have an awkward silence you could try to find some empathy. An example would be "I see you play cricket" to which the interviewer may reply "Yes I do, are you a cricketer."? Now, it gets tricky if you are not a cricketer, but a suitable reply would be "No, but I love watching cricket" or "No, but I'm interested in it and would like to take it up at some point"

It is in the interviewer's interest to get the best possible performance from you during an interview and a good interviewer should put you at ease. It is not in their interests for you to perform badly or to try and trip you up and catch you out. Interviewers practising this will often lose out on the possibility of gaining a good employee.

Most interviewers are aware of this and if you do get an interviewer who is trying to catch you out, remain calm and objective. They are the problem, not you, and you should question whether this is the right organisation for you. I have had interviews in the past where the interviewer's style put me off from taking a job. We all want equality and respect and if this can't be achieved before you have even started with an

Organisation then there is little chance of it happening once you have joined.

There will no doubt be questions you are unable to answer immediately. When this happens to buy some time – take a sip of water, if your interviewer has not given you any then use the water you have brought with you. It will, in any case, buy more time getting it out of your bag.

There are obvious time buyers, like repeating the question back to the panel before you answer or letting them know it is an interesting question. I think some Interviewers will see through that, but it is better to give a good well thought through answer than fumbling around trying to think of something to say.

A popular interview question is "where do you see yourself in five years?" This question gets asked as the interviewer will be trying to find out if you intend to stay with the organisation for any length of time or if you intend to leave and do something else. An example of what not to say would be "Running my own business" or "I intend to travel Europe at some point"

An ideal answer incorporates the goals of the

prospective organisation aligned to your own goals and consistent with the JD. So, in the case of, say, an Accountancy firm you could say, "I intend to qualify within the next two years and my ambition is to be promoted to Assistant Group Accountant within the new X division I understand you are setting up".

The second most popular question must be "can you tell me what your strengths and weaknesses are?" Personal and Professional strengths are relatively easy to run through and you align them to the role, making you the perfect fit. Weaknesses less so. The interviewer is asking this to see how honest you are in identifying your weaknesses.

When answering this question, always try and incorporate your action plan to resolve weaknesses. Here are a couple of examples:

- "I find it hard to delegate and take on too much, however, I recently attended a Project Management course, and I am implementing lessons learnt on the course. I now find that planning and allocating tasks at the start of a project leaves me free to project manage"
- "I love what I do and sometimes get too involved in a project resulting in my work/life balance

suffering, to overcome this I now make sure I leave work on time at least every other day. This has helped and made me more productive"

What you should be trying to do is turn a negative into a positive by starting the sentence with a positive, for example, "I love what I do", then the problem, in this case, work/life balance, then what you have done to resolve it, "leaving work early" and finally a benefit, "I'm more productive"

This brings us to the phrasing of your answers and specific words to use. If you have read the company's mission statement, it is a good idea to try and refer to it at some point and use words from the statement in some of your answers. This shows you are aligned to the organisation's ethos and goals.

In general, words, should be positive and upbeat, but not casual or slang. Instead of saying "I hope to" say "I intend to" it sounds more positive. It is common sense, but it is very easy to speak how you would normally talk and this is where recounting positive self-affirmations in a mirror can help.

Here are some words and phrases you may find useful

- I intend to…
- I have achieved
- I intend to achieve
- I am flexible
- I am highly committed
- I achieve results by …
- I am passionate about...
- I believe in….
- Diversity, Environment, Net Zero
- Teamwork, Team Player, Building, Fostering, Developing, Learning, Initiative
- Goals, Opportunity, Results
- Skills, Experience, Wealth of Knowledge
- World-Class, Award-Winning, Successful, Gold Standard
- Developed, Delivered, Won, Achieved, Initiative, Built, Maintained
- Enthusiasm, Energised, Love of, Motivated, Win-Win, Organised, Solution Orientated, Organised.

Whatever you say in an Interview make sure it is the truth, it is pointless embellishing a fact to the extent it becomes a lie. You will get found out sooner or later. Imagine stating you enjoy sailing, only to find out your new manager is a keen sailor and invites you out for a sailing day, but you get seasick.

We all have something unique in us which makes us special, and we do not need to lie or make ourselves look better than we are. Tell yourself you can do this on your own merit, and you will not need to lie. When discussing hobbies and interests steer clear of anything that could be considered controversial, better to play safe than enter controversy in an interview.

During the interview you will be allowed to ask questions, hopefully, you will have prepared these in advance and now is the time to refer to them. If during your interview some of the questions have been answered then cross these off and ask relevant questions only. If all the questions have been answered and you cannot think of any more, state a couple of the questions you were going to ask and say that these have been answered already so at this stage you have no further questions. It is fine to ask questions throughout the interview, and this shows you are engaged with the process. It is unusual to be asked to wait till the end of an interview to ask questions, but if this is the case then write the questions down as you think of them.

The type of questions you may want to ask are, how large the team is, what your duties would be, is the post new or are you replacing an existing employee, confirmation of your base, training programme and out of work facilities etc. etc.

Most interviews can last anywhere between half an hour to an hour. If you think yours has finished early, it may just be you have answered everything you can.

At the end of an interview, you may have a chance to "close the deal" by stating how grateful you are for the opportunity to be interviewed and ask if there is anything else you need to clarify. Assuming there is not, ask about the next steps and let them know you are very excited about the prospect of joining the organisation.

Second Interviews

"There are no shortcuts to any place worth going"

Beverley Sills

Some positions require a second interview, if you get one then that's great news. A second interview is a chance for the interviewer to clarify certain points and find out more about you, specifically they will be looking at what makes you a better candidate than the others. The interviewer will be trying to imagine working with you and if you will be a good fit within the team.

It is quite normal for there to be more than one person interviewing you. How you handle the second interview is the same as the first interview, don't let your guard down, although this interview may appear slightly more informal, it is still an interview. The chances are this interview will be harder than the first but shorter. Your interviewer has decided you meet the basic criteria above other candidates but now needs to make sure you are a perfect fit above those shortlisted, before making an offer.

Second Interviews may also include a tour of the workplace and an introduction to your team.

A second interview is a chance for the interviewer to drill down more closely into your experience and may include questions designed to test your knowledge, experience and how you would act in a certain situation.

From your first interview, you should have a good idea of the questions that may be asked, and you will have had time to prepare answers in advance so this should not pose a problem. It is however important that you have prepared further questions based on your first interview. Now is your opportunity to ask for more detail and specifics about the role and responsibilities.

You should expect to hear quite soon after your second interview if you have the job. Good signs are discussion of salary, perks, benefits and meeting the team.

Video Interviews

During COVID restrictions, many of us became used to working from home and conducting meetings through Video Conferencing tools. A natural progression from this, for many organisations, has been to move some interviews from a physical, in-person interview to a Video interview, at least during the initial stages of the process.

Video Interviews are not greatly different to an in-person interview, although you do not get the opportunity to physically see your workplace, however, you may be working remotely anyway.

The same basic principles apply to a video interview:

- Dress Appropriately
- Switch off phones, email and any distractions just before the interview starts
- Ensure that you have a neutral background
- Test your camera, speaker, microphone and connection before the start of the interview
- Conduct the interview in the same manner as you would if you were being physically interviewed
- Make sure that your background is neutral or blurred

Video Interviews can sometimes be shorter than you expect, so do not let this worry or put you off.

Other than that, the same principles of observation and answering questions apply.

Learning from the Process

"It's not whether you get knocked down, it's whether you get up"

Vince Lombardi

Not getting the job you want feels like rejection but sometimes it can be a blessing in disguise. Do not blame yourself, instead, try and learn from the process and run through the answers to the questions you gave. Analyse your performance in the interview, was it easy to answer questions or did you falter? What can you learn from the experience?

I believe most people have a fair idea of why they did not get a job and it is something we can learn from. You could try contacting the organisation and ask why you did not get the role and if there is anything you could have done better. Or you could ask your recruitment agent for feedback.

The important thing is to look at the positives, 1) you got an interview 2) your CV presents well because you got invited and you attended the interview and learnt 3) if you had a second interview then your first interview must have gone well.

Learning from the process and getting back up is a lesson we all must learn if we are to be happy and successful in our careers. If we are happy in our careers because we have made the right choices, then we will be successful.

If you have enjoyed reading this book please consider leaving a review.